——— *poems by* ———
K. JULIAN FLAMER

The
Canvas
Within

Reflections on Growth & Courage

The Canvas Within: Reflections on Growth & Courage
© 2025 by K. Julian Flamer

All rights reserved. No part of this publication may be reproduced, stored in a retrieval system, or transmitted in any form or by any means—electronic, mechanical, photocopying, recording, or otherwise—without the prior written permission of the copyright owner, except for brief quotations used in reviews, critical articles, or educational materials. This is a work of poetry and creative reflection. Names, places, and incidents are either the product of the author's imagination or are used fictitiously. Any resemblance to actual persons, living or dead, events, or locales is purely coincidental.

Published by **The 1 and Only Publishing Company**
4500 Forbes Blvd Lanham, MD 20706
Email: info@the1andonlypublishing.com
Website: www.the1andonlypublishing.com

Editing & Design: The 1 and Only Publishing Company
Cover Design & Interior Layout: The 1 and Only Publishing Design Team
Book Cover Illustrator: Chris Lyons

For more information on publishing your own book, visit
www.the1andonlypublishing.com.

ISBNs:
Paperback ISBN: **979-8-89741-024-8**
E-Book ISBN: **979-8-89741-025-5**

Printed in the United States of America
First Edition | 2025

For my father, Ken; my mother, Iris; and my sister, Lauren. Thank you for being my roots, my rhythm, and my reason.

CONTENTS

INTRODUCTION 1

BIO 3

GROWTH 5
    I Am 6
    Mistake 7
    Canvas 8
    Surf Foam 9
    Upside Down 10
    Calmer Mind 11
    Relentless 12
    Troubled Water 13
    Disappointment 14
    Ambitious Companion 15

LOVE 17
    Professor Failure 18

This Doesn't Feel Like Love Anymore 19
I Don't Want to Pick Up 20
She Saw Me 21
Katrina 22
We'll Try Again 24
Seen 25
Unnecessary Goodbye 26
Edge of Rise 27
Signify 28

CULTURE 29
U.S. 30
The Wait of the Hourglass 31
Parisian Irises Flowing North on Worth's Corner 32
Gift of Existence 33
Year's End 34
Expectations 35
Deep End of the Pool 36
To Be Heard 37
Impossible 38
Jump Start 39

LEGACY 41
Where Mother Meets God 42

Taurus Wagon 43

Familial Echoes 44

Principal 45

Quarter Century 46

Pop 48

Jado 49

Belmont Avenue 50

PJ 51

A Dream 52

COURAGE 53

The Shift 54

Fool 56

Start Over 57

Rut 58

Up Late 59

Anxious 60

Weekend Brothers 61

When We Get Up 62

Vocal Peace 63

Shadow 64

INTRODUCTION

The Canvas Within: Reflections on Growth & Courage is the debut poetry collection by K. Julian Flamer – it is a meditation on growth, love, legacy, culture and courage it takes to become.

From the quiet ache of memory to the loud joy of self-discovery, these poems trace the brushstrokes of a life shaped by both Northern roots and Southern soul.

This is a space for reflection. A mirror.
A beginning.
A return.
A canvas, painted with truth.

BIO

K. Julian Flamer is a poet forged by two worlds; Philadelphia, PA and Charlotte, NC. A former Dartmouth College football player turned actor with credits on network television shows and films, he brings a rare blend of discipline, emotional nuance, and narrative range to his work. His poetry navigates themes of identity, memory, transformation, and cultural duality.

GROWTH

"Do not go where the path may lead, go instead where there is no path and leave a trail"

— RALPH WALDO EMERSON

I AM

I am the buildup,
the weight beneath the breakthrough,
the silence before the shift.

Not polished, but combining
a mix of heat and breeze,
a draft that dared to lift.

I am bruised by the process,
bent by the lessons,
but better because I stood.

You see strength in the final product,
but I see it in the clay,
in the hands that shaped the shaping.

Every scar is a line in the story;
every pause was part of the pacing.
I am not made.
I am in the making.

MISTAKE

You published the words before you knew the title,
you stripped away the meaning before it was vital.
You acted heavy before you recognized the cost,
you blinked with no remorse and now your world is lost.
You arrived at an outcome before judging it's worth,
you sit around dreaming for an unlikely rebirth.
You pedal fast after the race is already over,
you're mad with regret from the place that you drove her.
You play it back differently, operating with more care,
you rest your sorrows on a far-reach dream and a prayer.
You pledge to be better only after you saw the outcome,
you think of a new day when you can finally say you got one.
You falsely reminisce because the present hurts so bad,
you look inward at your choices and overthink more than a tad.
You wonder why you strayed so harshly,
you strive for wholeness but settle with partially.
You know better now, and at least you take that away,
you silence the mind and watch the black lines turn grey.

CANVAS

Is it really pain or sport?
Is it only fast and short?
Is the past for us to sort?
Is the future for us to court?

Do we wake once we arrive?
Do we build purely off what's inside?
Do we grow off vision or to survive?
Do we have to bleed to be alive?

Can we step in the right direction?
Can we seek love over weak affection?
Can we accept another's complexion?
Can we fuel a deeper connection?

SURF FOAM

Let the thoughts come,
let the thoughts go.
Watch the clouds pass,
'til the sun rays show.

Let the words push,
let the words draw.
Watch the moon glow,
'til the dew falls

Let time hold its breath,
let the fear rest.
Watch the birds glide,
'til the next crest.

Let the light rise,
let the soul sing.
Watch the stars turn,
'til the stillness rings.

UPSIDE DOWN

At the end of the day,
you feel upside down,
turned around,
soul barely found.
Why so heavy?
We're called to suffer.
Ask yesterday,
you know who's tougher.
Friction filled,
corners dull,
edges whittled,
hardened skull.
At the end of the day,
you feel upside down,
mind your frown,
courage found.

CALMER MIND

There's a break in time,
between where you begin and when you grow.
Your thoughts heighten, but your drive slows,
a little less of an ideal dreamer,
and a little more of a realistic believer.

There's a break in time,
last winter's over and this winter's here.
Where your action slows more, but your priorities are clear.
Decisions to be made
and dues to be paid.

There's a break in time.
You're lost between where you thought you'd be and now,
where'd that motivation go, can't help but wonder how.
Reluctance and anxiety start knocking,
no stopping.

There's a break in time,
from stressful realizations to a calmer mind.
You've accepted what you came to find.
Never leave your goal
and always trust your soul.

RELENTLESS

I've learned that love can be unforgiving.
Compare what you got now to back then,
how's life worth living?
Time heals the heart but dries the wound.
Scars unfold and the memories bloom.

The center's sweet but the drug is sour
What can I, the human,
do with my power?
A couple weeks become a season,
years and years of missing and reason.

TROUBLED WATER

Fear can build up falsehood and strip down progress.
Fear can halt empowerment and kill momentum.
Fear can make hills from dust and place roadblocks on runways.
Fear doesn't love you.
Fear doesn't aid you.
Fear fears you.
Fear looks to change you.
Fear is a blessing;
without the darkness we can't find our illuminated path.
Fear is an answer;
without the question we can't know what we've learned.
Fear is a motive;
without the unchecked box, how can we know what we truly desire?
Fear wants you.
Fear needs you, but you don't need it, and it knows that.
Fear is a pillar of growth, an entryway of change.
Fear is a test, a journey.
Fear isn't real,
unless you make it so.

DISAPPOINTMENT

It bleeds through their words and tone.
It rips last night's smile off your face and punches you in the chest.
It's the frown, the self-loathing, and the crushing weight of failed expression.
The told you so's, the coulda shoulda woulda's.
"You can't have your cake and eat it too," she says.
Parental push, sibling sacrifice, personal persecution.
It breathes through your clouded sight,
a film to pull away before diving into the dream.
You walk through sand, over fire, underneath rain, amongst wind,
to get to where you can only see forward,
but it looks dark.
And the sun that was on your back has now faded and set.
"It's cold out there," he says,
but it's colder in here, in my center of feeling.
Desires slowly drip into regrets.
Passion justly retreats from where it recently showed its head.
You're empty, voided, ricocheted, crushed from within.

AMBITIOUS COMPANION

That which we want for ourselves,
becomes harder the faster we climb.
The further we reach,
it seems to be equally as far it is close.

Looking back and won'dring,
when we decided to step this way.
What motivated our first choice,
that's domino'ed all the others?

I see hope looking clearly,
but I see the shards of ice in between.
A pathway of decision making,
On the road to the greats.

LOVE

"Not until we are lost do we begin to understand ourselves"

— HENRY DAVID THOREAU

PROFESSOR FAILURE

You reach toward the fire and get charred.
You walk in the rain with no cover.
You settle for less and learn.
You begin to look the other

way more destructive now that you knew.
Way longer lasting than you thought.
Way less painful in the long run.
Way out of the sale with more than you caught

empty-handed before you tried.
Empty-handed before you could care
Empty-handed without a full-length lesson
Empty-handed before, but now more aware

of the possibilities on the other side,
of the love lost and discovered anew,
of the potential that's nearly reached,
of the discovery inside your view.

THIS DOESN'T FEEL LIKE LOVE ANYMORE

I felt matched, I felt mirrored.
Now we just take, I feel triggered.

It was you and me versus them all.
We had each other, our own cabal.

Now I reach and you're not there.
No soft cheek, no chestnut hair.

No summer smile, no freckled face.
All love is gone, rank aftertaste.

I DON'T WANT TO PICK UP

She once touched my heart,
fingers between my feelings,
my thoughts laid in her hands.

Behind my eyes,
tapping the deep corners of my soul,
she heard me in the dark.
I breathed my truth onto her mental palette,
lines for shapes with open spaces
filled with the color of our moments.
And now those once damp canals
of that so recent memory
have dried to something barren and stale.

Where the elixir thickened as it flowed,
as it once soothed those channels,
it now clots them.
Going back is driving fast on bald tires
to a place that no longer exists,
to a spark that no longer catches.

SHE SAW ME

A tear that fell for the first time
in a decade unlocked by heartbreak and feeling the loss
of decisions that clouded,
and cost me.
For I wished it wasn't,
until I saw the lessons of truth and honor,
where fate didn't let me slide.
Through that moment,
I now saw what she saw
and got scared to look up.
But what I finally touched
was my new form,
fulfilled by passion.
She saw me there,
but I rose too late.
Now my scar has healed, thick,
a wide keloid.
I will wear it and carry,
my burden.

KATRINA

The door cracked, creaked, and then split open revealing lush, rich, cherry-wood hair, pulled back for work mode.

Her eyes crossed over the human horizon of faces until glossing over my awe.
Blue eyes, too crystal for sky and too dreamy for sea; a heartbeat, a skip, and then another... were only my soles grounded?

Perfect lips, dark pink and begging to be worshiped; three open buttons down into two sun- soaked precious lumps of possibility and down a well-monitored abdominal region.

Hips tucked business into a sophisticated pencil skirt with God-blessed curves, and presumably the best pink lady apple you've ever seen behind it all.

A knee to thigh ratio that screamed of a four-day-a-week mid-distance runner.

A set of stiletto pumps supporting her constant mission.

An energy that screamed power, lust, and pure desire from Southern California's highest hill and into its deepest canyon.

Her light reflective of a rare dwarf star's.

She then cocked her head 45 degrees, laughing at another classmate's sidebar joke; I was so consumed that I missed the social part of the exchange.

You climb a mountain and yell at its tippy-top, you numbly sprint through a marathon finish line, you land after a 19-hour cross world flight; the pleasure and release can't hold a note to this beautiful symphony.

Ten seconds of heart-halting, jaw-sinking, eye-grazing discovery... "Hi, I'm Katrina, I don't think we've met," she said.

We may have, in some existential set of hope and longing, where fantasy comes closer to reality. We must use our humanly efforts to bring them together.

I had seen beauty, I had seen perfection; but none seemed to measure up to what this was, this was more of a fate situation, an answer of prayers if you will.

My eyes were panting. My hand extended, she gripped it hard to make sure I recognized the exchange: ball in my court.

Time to figure out a way to score, her.

WE'LL TRY AGAIN

I walked away toward another day.
It ended,
a cliché.
Reverse foreplay.

We grew apart
by trust and by heart.
Moments I can't outsmart.
Erase the flowchart.

Could come back around,
a spark re-found.
That memorable sound,
love-story bound.

SEEN

After the first several layers,
comes the fruit.
What's within makes up the root,
a drive that's luscious and captivating,
a style that's rugged and motivating.

Discovering what makes up the defaults,
a power that's stronger than rock salt.
The slow smile that creeps as she learns more
of your purpose, the one that she dives for.

Once respected, then admired,
opens the heart, partner acquired.
After the first several layers, comes the fruit.
What's within makes up the root.

UNNECESSARY GOODBYE

I still sense my palms pressing down your cheeks
I still smile when you do.
I still feel the echo of shared mornings
I still laugh with you too.
I still want to tell you what I've seen
I still yearn to walk by your outer shoulder on the sidewalk.
I still feel pain because we lost
I still replay my moves wondering why.
I still wake thinking of you
I still look at the past as if it's mendable.
I still play out what I might say
I still try to fathom what could've been.
I still want a different ending
I still settle with an unnecessary goodbye.

EDGE OF RISE

You ever feel on the brink
of something great,
but it's only love and hate?

Stop, go, don't, no,
but you know you can make
a turn any day towards a break.

You ever hear something's there
but you're out of risks,
tired of being a rag doll to twist?

Wanna keep a head up,
don't let up, make it burn.
No retreat, no return.

SIGNIFY

I feel my mind's eye cry.
I'm disappointed
I yearn for reasons why.
I want to signify
and my soul cannot be shy.
How can my dreams
and my reality emulsify?

CULTURE

"Man is pushed by drives. But he is pulled by values"

— VIKTOR FRANKL

U.S.

The state of America is more than just one us,
it encompasses and relates to all of us.
From leaders who don't acknowledge us,
to police who won't let us,
to oppressors who don't see us,
to internationals who no longer want to be us.
It's about the news, who won't believe us,
leaders who look to deceive us,
to bigots who see to unweave us,
knowing damn well what we can achieve, us.
Colors of beauty, why demean us?
We are all beautiful and bright. Choose to accept us.
We are running in protest like orphans; you should've kept us.
We pray to God to intercept us.
They choose to hate.
But not us.

THE WAIT OF THE HOURGLASS

Like healing wounds,
things deepen before they mend.
The passing of time
becomes sand between seasons;
the grains of becoming
color our moments
and flavor our milestones,
spilling time.

But there's faith in falling sand
and gain in tilted truth.
Those same winds
that rush through your worry
flow through the harvest
of becoming.

PARISIAN IRISES FLOWING NORTH ON WORTH'S CORNER

Imagine a wind so strong it carries memories
and connects them with possibilities,
further into reality, a French corner.
We speak of the blissful places as if we recognize
the awe that lies ahead of you.
We've heard of their wines and breads and cheeses and smiles.
yet the difference is that you will savor
wide boulevards, extravagant fashion,
cathedrals, cafes, boutiques, and passion.
Right around worth's corner,
discovery will lessen the blow and enhances the mind.
Architecture devised with love,
food prepared with care,
a genuine essence and a compassionate breeze,
the absorption and acceptance of life's real happiness.
Escape the western bubble; enrich your near-pure soul
See our international downfalls,
see their intra-national love circle.
Grow, become, change, bring back.
Seek out with a permeable mind
and take note with a conscious heart and a tenured ear
of the beauty right around worth's corner.

GIFT OF EXISTENCE

My existence is perpetuated by what I've done,
who I've known,
where I've been, how,
I've changed.
Not by a thing, a physical holding or offering,
it is my existence that marks my place in time.
Giving should be of the soul, not by the eye,
a return of energies between presentation and application.
Gifting season becomes a quantity battle of what you can gain
rather than a quality engagement of how you can grow.
My light shines because you've given me oil,
not because you've changed out the bulb.
My essence grows not because you've filled my basket,
but because you've embraced my heart.
My mind travels because you've shown me where it can go,
Not because you've taken me there.

A season for care, not for comfort,
A time for love, not for pleasure,
A moment of beauty not a trade.
This gift holds endless weight and beauty.

YEAR'S END

Troubled, we can't help but be.
Scarred, so much that we may never see.
Battered, by some of the choices.
Crushed, our hearts and voices.
Changed, to become better versions.
Motivated, for new excursions.
Pressured, to apply and strive.
Cleared, for newer days to arrive.
Weathered, but now we the people thrive.
Rooted, yet reaching toward the sky.
Awakened, for the next generation to deal.
Bettered, for our old ones to heal.

EXPECTATIONS

We're impatient, so we jump the gun.
We're hesitant, so we miss the fun.

We're restless because it's not fair,
We're scared because we've been there.

We lack understanding because we think we're better.
We regret because we're destined to be go-getters.

We perceive it at its worst.
We want our number drawn first.

We've missed our blessing.
We've failed our testing.

We expect because we deserve.
We anticipate because we long to be heard.

We yearn for more
and we miss what's in store.

DEEP END OF THE POOL

We're never really prepared.
Three steps ahead lives perfection.
Action beats ready.
To jump is to grow is to win.
We defer to others who we think are different
or better
or able,
when we all start behind the line.
Some jump,
some climb,
some stay static.
Some play fantasy,
but dipping in means eventually falling,
and falling means future-you will catch present-you,
and the drop becomes the gift.

TO BE HEARD

I gather my thoughts,
not rehearsed, but real.
An impression, a reflection, a reveal
of who I am, who I was, who I might be:
a dreamer,
carrying raw, unfiltered sensitivity.
I've guarded it with muscle,
defended it with words,
but at the core,
I am nothing more
than one who yearns for the hurdle.
The people, the places,
those metaphorical races,
they pull me forward.
They keep me still.
So I listen,
I observe
this beautiful, spinning gift of a world
until I'm heard.

IMPOSSIBLE

Look out, over, and off the cliff to the edge of where fear sits.
Backed up against a sharp corner, whose other side is bliss and pride.
Similar in intensity but opposite in tension,
one yanks us away while one nudges us lovingly closer
to what our make-up is made of.
Sometimes the chest thumps out of excitement
because our inner self can taste that other side,
but this side is what we've really known
until the limit becomes the starting block,
until the ceiling becomes the floor,
until the window becomes the doorway
and we can cash in on our agreement with life.
To uphold our side as she upholds hers,
where we challenge one another
until life maketh the man and experience maketh the story,
until perception maketh what we see,
until perspective maketh when we start,
until discernment maketh how we rise.

JUMP START

The daily grind is our universal truth,
the pre-American dream.
The thin line between where we stand
and higher self-esteem.
Wanting what we don't have
and taking for granted what's already there,
always looking to level up
and find another way to compare.

Blink and miss a blessing.
Fall and miss a ledge.
Status is based on recovery.
Adversity brings our edge.

LEGACY

"Keep your nose in the wind,
and your eye along the skyline"

— DEL GUE IN JEREMIAH JOHNSON

WHERE MOTHER MEETS GOD

Where principle meets change,
where style meets grace,
where words meet respect,
where class meets taste,
that's mother.

When age meets reflection,
when drive meets destination,
when practice meets perfect,
when hard work meets anticipation,
that's mother.

Why life catches up,
why reluctance goes down,
why morals stay steady,
why it all comes around,
that's mother.

Where strength meets power,
where manners meet others,
where mother meets God,
and God meets mother.

TAURUS WAGON

Early words
outside of school before jumping out,
and leaning in.
He said, "Be affable, Dutch,
light-skinned or not."
I had to stand up straighter,
and fight harder
for my place
in a place without a place for me.
He said, "Be gregarious, Dutch,
lift your hand high to be called on,
show them a hoss.
And a young man of mission,
Of strength."

FAMILIAL ECHOES

You ever smile through the phone
and the words feel like home?
Familiar laughs,
felt pain,
the ache of being far.
You want to be near.
You want to be there,

You're built by the ones who raised you,
drained by the ones who pay you.
You want your shine to honor them,
your wins to ripple home.

PRINCIPAL

It wasn't *yeah*, it was *yes*.
It wasn't luck, I was blessed.
It wasn't *try*, it was *do*.
It wasn't can't, my mother knew.

Fundamentals that paid me
Scriptures that saved me.
Appreciation she gave me
Boy to man, she made me.

I'll always remember to be aware of her hands
Strong and determined, with the experience of lands.
I'll always be aware of her luxurious smile
Soft and genuine, it got me through every mile.

It took time to learn lessons, to find my truth
She gave me the gift of life, sacrificed for my youth.
Made me steadily aware and always on time
pushed me to be better, made sure I was first in line.

At the end of the teens, right before manhood,
she always knew best, she always heard me.
I salute you, I thank God for you
My backbone, always there through and through.

QUARTER CENTURY

At one I slobbered and blinked; my sister gave me the nickname "Bink".
At two I grew from fat nugget to chubby baby, yelling for mommy to save me.
At three I began to speak, mouthing words and turning cheeks.
At four I wanted more, looked up to book bags and preschool floors.
At five I was up to bat with a yellow pencil and a stylish sailor's hat.
At six I first got sick, my immune system learned how to kick.
At seven I was a big shot, new bunk beds and a plastic watch.
At eight I knew it all, sat waiting while you looked for sales in the King of Prussia mall.
At nine I ferociously swam, learned competition and early stages of being a man.
At ten I donned cargo pants and soccer sneaks, picked up sitcoms and a love for the beach.
At eleven we headed south, rural streets and a twang to the mouth.
At twelve I wanted my own, a big room and a blue house phone.
At thirteen I had a mind, started seeing girls and establishing kinds.
At fourteen I was extroverted, sleepovers at Taylor's and some poor behavior alerted.
At fifteen I had big dreams, high school parties and new teams.
At sixteen I thought I was grown, went from JV to varsity, house to cell phone.
At seventeen I started thinking college, double-timed my act and yearned for knowledge.
At eighteen it was time to move on, to challenge all my lessons and stay strong.
At nineteen I discovered the style of New York, started clubbing and popping corks.

At twenty I missed home, was tired of relentless football and feeling alone.
At twenty-one I made it to the Ivy League, cleaned up my act and became intrigued.
At twenty-two I played my last season, frat memories and the official age of reason.
At twenty-three I parked back home, discovered film acting and began to roam.
At twenty-four I headed west, found my warm home base and became obsessed.
At twenty-five I look back on it all; the wounds, the wins, the highs, the flaws.

POP

There exists a level of clarity that only comes from a father.
A way to lighten the hammer blows of life, so they no longer bother.
A calmness that hits your heart when it needs it most,
true power in divine guidance, a primal dose.
Foresight and experience touch in the middle,
clear-cut perspective, no falsehoods or riddles.
He powers my drive, he fuels my mood
He'll tell it to me straight, however blunt, however crude.
We sit in the backroom and tell stories to compare.
We plot our next moves; we progress and arrive square.
They say what birthed you is what will stick 'til the end,
much more than a parent, much more than a friend.
Talks with Pop last late, surpass the night
with words to rest my soul on; I'll take on life ready to fight.

JADO

Always there to uplift,
always there with grace,
embraced by siblingship,
the one true embrace.

My loving sister,
brilliant with care,
effervescently seeking,
my life-given prayer.

Dynamic and sharp
extraordinary and bright.
I fell and she caught me,
my guiding light.

With an outspoken heart
and a soul that won't sway,
she speaks truth with courage
and clears clouds from my day.

BELMONT AVENUE

When I envision my earliest realizations of strength and pride,
I see Alice Hines.
She walked with me at my most vulnerable,
told me to stand tall, be humble and kind.
My words always held true to the manners and maturity she expected.
Always a grasp away, I was never falsely directed.
She raised a team of survivors and teachers,
who yearn to reach more divine places,
Spiritually grounded siblings with dreamer minds and chiseled faces.
A time or two I said, "I can't", but she showed me that I can.
Those school days at the bus stop, rain or shine, we walked hand-in-hand.
As your beautiful soul lays to heavenly rest,
I wish you love, relief,
and a transition blessed.

P J

Level up and do better.
It's time, Jules. It's time.
Be abundant in your preparation
and understand your plan.
Communicate like a man,
so masterful,
deterrents hate to say you can.
Make the world understand.
Don't buy, create with your hand.
Push yourself,
each day make a fan.
So, what's your goal?
Decide and rely.
Move wildly through the sky.
Party on until you die.

A DREAM

A dream is where we part.
Surety, the liquid of the heart.
Quietly, is how it always starts.

Moving, so we can begin.
Foresight, with all your kin.
Excited, throw caution to the wind.

Blossom, as you push it on.
Freedom, keeps it strong.
Flavor, carries it along.

A dream starts with a thought.
Pushes, past where it's caught.
Live, and let it be taught.

COURAGE

"A man's worth is no greater
than the worth of his ambitions"

— MARCUS AURELIUS

THE SHIFT

We've all been there
The late nights, the long strides,
going over and above
because something inside said, "You must".
But somewhere along the timeline,
the grind gets quieted,
muted by bills,
softened by couches and contentment.
It feels good to stop.
To breathe.
To let the world keep spinning
while you stay still.
But stillness is not soul.
Stillness is pause.
Essence lives in the forward.
In friction.
In the fire of the next step.
Remember momentum?
It was loud in grade school halls,
it roared into dorm rooms,
Or into those dreams that never needed diplomas
It was ours
until young adulthood dulled it.
Until comfort sold us safety.
Until we picked careers
that fit like quiet lies
instead of tailored truths.

But momentum
didn't die.
It dulled.
It hid.
It broke and bled,
But it never left.
It waits
in the background of our breath,
in the corner of conviction.

And the beautiful thing?
It's changeable.
Reclaimable.
Reachable.
Because this is not a fable.
Not space.
Not scripted.

This is real.
Where choices count
and courage calls,
the spark?
It just shifts
And today, it could be yours.

FOOL

It happened.
It happened again.
Where's the relief?
I thought we were friends.
I was supposed to be good.
This can't be the end.
Time won't stop ticking.
I want to ascend.

START OVER

"The magic you're seeking is in the work you're avoiding," they say.
The moment my ambition meets action will be my heyday.
As opening your mind carries the tools to build your cabin,
 as sacrificing for your deepest desire can lead to all that you imagined

"If it costs you your peace, it's too expensive," they said,
 but peace is relative to your path; stone turns to diamond instead.
When the circle is tight, but your outlook is wider,
 your present fuels your future and choice becomes the divider.

RUT

I'm in a rut that's not so fine,
I'm in a rut to pass the time.
I hope it leaves but unless I push,
my yearning become a burning bush.
I'm in a rut that leaves me worried,
I can feel my dreams; I should've hurried.
I want for more, I know I have it,
time for routines to become better habits.
I'm in a rut, I'm better than this,
I know myself; I want my bliss.
I see it clear, so very near,
it's fear keeping me nestled here
I'm in a rut, I want out now,
God gave me talent; I'm stuck on how.
I want that medal, I want that win,
I'm made for it, I know I can swim.
I'm in a rut, but I'm breaking out,
I'm too good for this, I can't allow the pout.
I will go there, I will be heard,
I will make moves, I'm heaven's bird.

UP LATE

I once again find myself up late,
past dipping and future diving,
circling my mind.
For a moment, I've been great,
rhyme plotting and dream grinding,
my pushed passion through words is no mistake.
Hook mining and fantasy finding
tying plans to wins I don't self-hate,
I once again
find myself up late.

ANXIOUS

Apparently, I'm stuck in the past,
wondering if this tight chest will last.
It could've happened so many other ways,
but instead, my present comfort pays.

Apparently, I'm looking to the future.
Maybe my thoughts will be sutures,
or maybe they'll betray and drop me back down.
The worry that once blew away, has come back around.

Apparently, I'm avoiding my present,
hoping for a better sense of pleasant.
"Nothing else matters," they say.
When will this suffering roll away?

Apparently, I'm a victim of my mind.
Stuck between up there and behind.
My peace wavering, compromised.
My flow overthought, overanalyzed.

WEEKEND BROTHERS

Plans slowly build to an eventual compromise,
a shared desire for pouring in and pouring
out. While channeling care-free-freedom,
we lock knuckles and wrap shoulders.
Smiles emerge and relief flows
off our backs like water beads on duck feathers
'til it drips down into a pit of camaraderie,
the same pit that kept Peter Pan young.
And while it wastes, we wonder
if this is what brotherhood was meant to be
or if time is just burning out
like a wide-wicked candle
that flickers as we keep our flames high,
as night pours in

and the energy halts.

WHEN WE GET UP

We miss.
We fault.
We lack.
We fail.
We stop.
We won't.
We can't.
We don't.
But we cancel out the above
when we get up.
We cry.
We bleed.
We rip.
We stain.
We hurt.
We harden.
We wither.
We hurt.
We hurt.
But we overcome
when we get up.

VOCAL PEACE

First, hear your voice.
Then dare to speak it.
If you feel doubt,
let your spirit lead it.
Can you be brave?
Can you receive it,
the purpose,
the pull,
the truth once you believe it?
Be proud of it.
Let want ignite motion
let motion define.
Don't run from it,
stand in your power,
speak with the divine.
Decide on it,
if believe is a seed,
then action must grow.
I still hold that lesson deep in my soul.

SHADOW

I've moved in the dark,
tried to rewrite the past,
a losing illusion.
But light began to break t
hrough habits I reshaped.
I questioned my motives,
the core of my character,
and traced old reasons why,
then shifted their weight.
I've moved in the dark.

EVERY CANVAS TELLS A STORY.

IF THESE WORDS SPOKE TO YOURS, STAY **CONNECTED**.

Stay connected to future writings, events, and projects that celebrate the art of becoming.

Scan to join Julian's circle

and receive words that move beyond the page.

www.ingramcontent.com/pod-product-compliance
Lightning Source LLC
Chambersburg PA
CBHW070550090426
42735CB00013B/3144